P9-CFN-743

Squirrel Kits

by Ruth Owen

Consultants:
Suzy Gazlay, M.A.
Recipient, Presidential Award
for Excellence in Science Teaching

Leah Birmingham, RVT
Assistant Director
Sandy Pines Wildlife Centre
Napanee, Ontario, Canada

BEARPORT
PUBLISHING

New York, New York

Credits
Cover and title page, © Kassia Halteman/Shutterstock; 4–5, © C.C. Lockwood/Animals Animals; 7T, © Shutterstock; 7B, © Cappi Thompson/Shutterstock; 8–9, © Shutterstock; 10, © Joseph Scott Photography/Shutterstock; 11, © Robert Canis/FLPA; 12–13, © S & D & K Maslowski/FLPA; 14, © Color-Pic Inc./Animals Animals; 15, © Kassia Halteman/Shutterstock; 16–17, © Doug Wechsler/Animals Animals; 18, © Shutterstock; 19, © Charles F. McCarthy/Shutterstock; 20, © S. Cooper Digital/Shutterstock; 21, © Joe Gough/Shutterstock; 22T, © Paula Cobleigh/Shutterstock; 22B, © Shutterstock; 23T, © Cappi Thompson/Shutterstock; 23C, © Robert Canis/FLPA; 23B, © C.C. Lockwood/Animals Animals.

Publisher: Kenn Goin
Editorial Director: Adam Siegel
Creative Director: Spencer Brinker
Design: Alix Wood
Photo Researcher: Ruby Tuesday Books Ltd

Library of Congress Cataloging-in-Publication Data

Owen, Ruth, 1967–
  Squirrel kits / by Ruth Owen.
     p. cm. — (Wild baby animals)
  Includes bibliographical references and index.
  ISBN-13: 978-1-61772-160-1 (library binding)
  ISBN-10: 1-61772-160-3 (library binding)
  1. Squirrels—Infancy—Juvenile literature. I. Title.
  QL737.R68O94 2011
  599.36'2139—dc22
                                2010041250

Copyright © 2011 Bearport Publishing Company, Inc. All rights reserved. No part of this publication may be reproduced in whole or in part, stored in any retrieval system, or transmitted in any form or by any means, electronic, mechanical, photocopying, recording, or otherwise, without written permission from the publisher.

For more information, write to Bearport Publishing Company, Inc., 101 Fifth Avenue, Suite 6R, New York, New York 10003. Printed in the United States of America in North Mankato, Minnesota.

122010
10810CGE

10 9 8 7 6 5 4 3 2 1

Contents

Meet some squirrel kits

Two baby squirrels are having fun in the trees.

The babies are called **kits**.

They run along branches.

They leap from tree to tree.

The babies are playing chase!

4

Squirrel kits

All about squirrels

Many kinds of squirrels live in trees.

Gray squirrels have gray or black fur with white bellies.

Other kinds have red fur with white bellies.

Adult squirrel size

Red fur

All squirrels have long, **bushy** tails.

Bushy tail

Gray squirrel

Where do squirrels live?

Squirrels live in almost every part of the world.

Some live in forests and parks.

Others live in towns and cities.

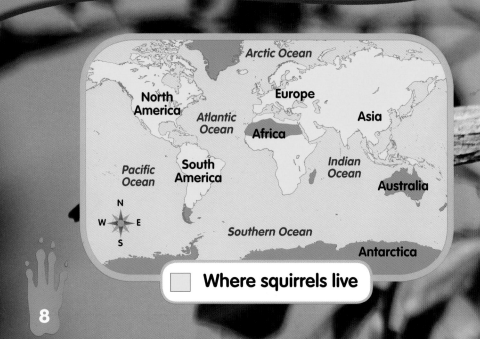

Where squirrels live

Gray squirrel

Lots of gray squirrels live in North America.

Squirrel homes

Gray squirrels build homes called **dreys**.

They build their dreys high up in the trees.

A drey is made out of twigs and leaves.

A squirrel puts feathers, leaves, and dry grass inside to make it soft and warm.

Drey

Mothers and kits

A mother gray squirrel makes a nest in a hole in a tree.

She gives birth to her kits in the nest.

Sometimes she gives birth in a drey.

The kits' eyes are closed, so they cannot see.

They also have no fur.

The mother feeds the kits milk from her body.

Kits feeding

Mother squirrel

13

Squirrel kits

After a few weeks, the kits open their eyes.

Now they can see.

Their fur grows, too.

The kits first go outside their nest or drey when they are about seven weeks old.

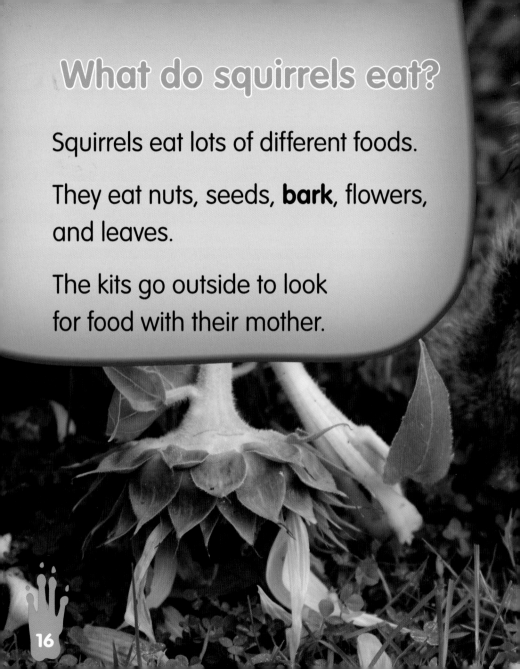

What do squirrels eat?

Squirrels eat lots of different foods.

They eat nuts, seeds, **bark**, flowers, and leaves.

The kits go outside to look for food with their mother.

Sunflower

Clever squirrels

In the fall, squirrels collect extra food.

They **bury** it in the ground.

When winter comes, there's less food around.

So squirrels dig up the food they buried in the fall and eat it.

Squirrel burying food

Sometimes squirrels steal
the nuts and seeds that
people feed to birds!

19

The kits grow up

The kits leave their mother when they are about three months old.

They find their own food.

They build their own dreys.

The kits are ready to begin their grown-up lives!

Glossary

bark (BARK) the tough covering on the outside of a tree

bury (BER-ee) to make a hole in the ground, put something inside, and then cover it over

bushy (BUSH-ee) thick and fluffy

dreys (DRAYZ) homes that squirrels make using twigs and leaves

kits (KITS) the babies of some animals, such as squirrels and skunks

Index

Read more

Diemer, Lauren. *Squirrels (Backyard Animals).* New York: Weigl (2008).

Lundgren, Julie K. *Squirrels (Life Cycles).* Vero Beach, FL: Rourke (2011).

Swanson, Diane. *Squirrels (Welcome to the World of Animals).* New York: Gareth Stevens (2003).

Townsend, Emily Rose. *Squirrels (Woodland Animals).* Mankato, MN: Capstone (2004).

Learn more online

To learn more about squirrels,
visit **www.bearportpublishing.com/WildBabyAnimals**

About the author

Ruth Owen has been writing children's books for more than ten years. She lives in Cornwall, England, just minutes from the ocean. Ruth loves gardening and caring for her family of llamas.